Special Thanks

Our special thanks goes to Mikhail Brown whose tireless efforts at editing, screening, computer assisting and eight months of total dedication made this book a reality.

International Standard Book Number: 0-9648948-1-5
Library of Congress Catalog Card Number: 95-092552

First Edition
Printed in the United States of America.

Acknowledgements

The following people and organizations were very cooperative in supplying technical assistance, advice, encouragement and inspiration:

Hohner, Inc.
Mikhail Brown
Virginia Glenn
Fred Morris, President Maxx Records, Nashville, Tennessee
James Tiller, recording artist
The Society for the Preservation & Advancement of the Harmonica
Robin Cook

Dedication

This book is dedicated to those part-time musicians who never get to ride the Greyhounds to gigs, to see the spotlight, their name on an album, or make it to the big time. It's dedicated to the butchers, carpenters, janitors, teachers, and others who on Friday and Saturday nights become weekend musicians in the bars, honky tonks, dancehalls, and rough houses across America.

It is also dedicated to our children whom we love dearly - Steven Gerard, Natalie Brynne and Bethany Shanel.

Illustrations

Illustrated by Sharon & Ray Steelman. Unless otherwise indicated photographs are by David Brown Photography or Phillip D. Sanders of Huntsville, Alabama.

Edited by:

Dr. Glenda Moody, PhD.   Scottsboro, Alabama
Mikhail J. Brown   Huntsville, Alabama

ABOUT THE AUTHORS

Ray and Sharon Steelman are a husband and wife team living in New Market, Alabama. They have had several publications to their credit. Most of these publications deal with educational research or the technical aspects of employee benefit programs, which is their principal occupation. Listed below are some of their private works and publications.

A Short Study of Industrial Education in the United States   1970

A Curriculum Guide for Female Industrial Arts Students   1971

A Study of Safety Hazards in Public Secondary Schools in Middle Tennessee   1972

A Curriculum Guide for Architectural Drawing Students in Public Secondary Schools in Huntsville, Alabama   1974

Learn to Play the Harmonica (Book & Cassette)   1978

It's Not Easy Being Me (Collection of Poems)   1985

The Mechanics of Self-funding   1989

Legal Forms for the Insurance Executive   1991

Add a Room...Up   1991

Learn to Play the Harmonica...Nashville Style   1991

In addition to the above, the authors have been published in several insurance trade magazines including Broker World, Life Insurance Selling, Life and Health Insurance Sales, Health Insurance Underwriter and the Alabama Health Underwriters Newsletter. A home remodeling project resulted in the short story, Add a Room...Up, a summary of which was published in Home Mechanix magazine. Some of their poetry has been published in The Sampler, a quarterly publication of poetry by the Alabama State Poetry Society. For several years the Steelmans published a monthly employee benefit newsletter, the Update, which circulated to employers throughout North Alabama and South Tennessee.

The Steelmans work primarily as business consultants in areas of employee benefits, corporate insurance, and estate planning for executives. They also are perfect examples of the entrepreneural spirit as founders and owners of three businesses: Professional Benefit Management, OccuDent Dental Plans, and Steelman Music Enterprises. In 1979, when their first harmonica book and tape, Learn to Play the Harmonica, was published, it was found to be an overwhelming success. The demand for a more advanced text led to the publication of <u>Learn to Play the Harmonica...Nashville Style</u> in 1991.

Ray began playing the harmonica after being inspired by Charlie McCoy who, along with his band, the Escorts, played at a high school dance in Fayetteville, Tennessee in 1962. Charlie's influence is obvious in the musical arrangements and the style music that Ray plays. When listening to Ray's playing, you also will find traces of licks and riffs from Jelly Roll Johnson, Terry McMillan, Jimmie Fadden, Mickey Rafael, and "Fingers" Taylor. An occasional lick from the blues influence of Little Walter and Peter "Madcat" Ruth might also be detected. This potpourri of styles and techniques blend into a delightful combination of the "Nashville-style harmonica" sound.

Ray is not a "full-time" professional musician although he did play "seven days a week" for several years "in the trenches" of the clubs, taverns and bars from Nashville to Birmingham and is currently a member of the American Federation of Musicians Local No. 257 in Nashville, Tennessee. Today, most of his playing time is spent in the recording studios of North Alabama playing "backup" on demonstration tapes for songwriters and aspiring new stars. Ray has made numerous guest appearances at performing arts festivals, state and county fairs, state parks and major theme parks including Opryland USA and Looney's Entertainment Park. In competition he has won numerous titles in bluegrass and fiddlers' conventions across Alabama and Tennessee. In one recent year, Ray simultaneously held the harmonica titles of Alabama State Champion, Tennessee Valley Bluegrass Champion, Tennessee Valley Champion and was first runner up for the Tennessee State Championship. In 1991, Ray released two very successful harmonica cassette albums, <u>Loco Motion</u> and <u>Hyperventilation Blues</u>. In 1993, two more cassette albums followed. They were Harp Attack and Ray Steelman and The Good, the Bad and the Ugly...Live. Ray Steelman's Bama Jammer tape was released in the Fall of 1994.

In the Summer of 1995, the Steelmans produced two harmonica video instructional guides. These along with all of their other publications and audio tapes may be found in most music stores, book stores, tourist attractions and theme parks.

CONTENTS

INTRODUCTION

Many people are under the impression that the harmonica is a child's toy, an instrument that can be mastered easily and quickly; normally, this is not true. There is no easy way to learn to do anything well, and to play the harmonica well requires as much time, dedication and practice as does any other musical instrument.

We have now seen the harmonica come into its own as almost all country, blues, pop, folk and rock music has a "harp" written into it. Today's professionals have learned to produce extremely complicated music from a simple diatonic harmonica. The techniques of bending, choking, crossing [see Picker's Glossary, page 3], and even straight harmonica playing are sometimes so difficult that only the best musicians can master them. So, do not expect to play like the professionals unless you are willing to put in a great deal of practice.

It has been estimated that today over 40 million people in the United States play the harmonica, out of which over $1^{1}/_{2}$ million claim to be experts. In the U.S. there are more harmonicas than all other musical instruments combined. People who play the harmonica range from children to the elderly, senators to housewives, and astronauts to presidents.

The popularity of the harmonica is not limited to the United States. France, for example, holds a contest each year to elect a "Miss Harmonica." It is estimated that over 4,000 harmonica bands exist throughout the world. China boasts that it is home to "the best" harmonica players in the world. The International Harmonica Federation has members from more than 40 countries. Today, it is possible for music students to earn a college degree in harmonica at some universities in the United States. New York's City College became the first institution of higher learning to implement a major in harmonica as a degree program. In 1948, the American Federation of Musicians recognized the harmonica as a legitimate instrument. Today, the organization lists thousands of harmonicists on its national membership roster.

In joining the ranks of today's harmonica players, you will become a part of an old and large family. You will have a constant companion in your harmonica no matter where life takes you. While listening to music you will find that you hear "harp licks" even when they are not there; that you have turned into a "thief" stealing "riffs" anytime you can; and that you do not just play the harmonica - it has become part of you!

LEARNING CURVE

When you first start playing the harmonica you learn everything to which you are exposed because all the material is new. Your learning curve looks like this:

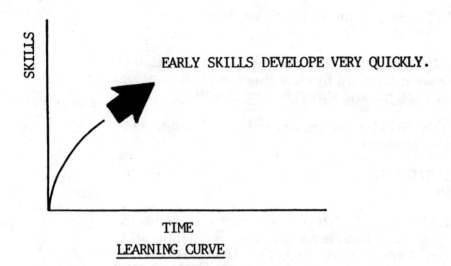

EARLY SKILLS DEVELOPE VERY QUICKLY.

TIME

LEARNING CURVE

After learning the basic skills, breathing patterns, straight playing and a few special effects, a person's progress begins to slow down. Normally, when a player starts learning the difficult skills (bending, crossing, etc.) progress slows to a crawl. This is why there are so few highly skilled harmonica players - most never get past this "wall." They become discouraged, practice less and finally discard the harp or give it to one of their children. Persistence makes professionals and you simply have to hang in there!

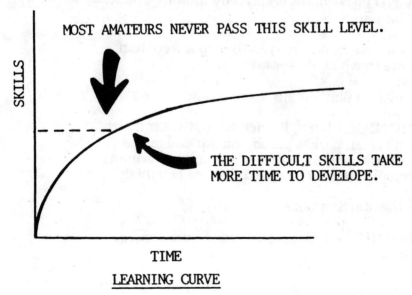

MOST AMATEURS NEVER PASS THIS SKILL LEVEL.

THE DIFFICULT SKILLS TAKE MORE TIME TO DEVELOPE.

TIME

LEARNING CURVE

THE PICKER'S GLOSSARY

Before you go any further, you need to familiarize yourself with the following terms:

BEAT - the rhythm to which you tap your foot in time with music.

BENDING or CHOKING - changing the pitch of a note downward by changing the air flow across your tongue and through your mouth.

BLOW NOTES - notes created by exhaling, or breathing out.

CHORDING - playing several notes at the same time.

CROSS HARMONICA - playing a harmonica in a key other than the tonic chord (key) [playing a "C" harmonica in the key of "G"; playing a "D" harmonica in the key of "A"; etc.]. Cross playing normally refers to 2nd position playing.

DIATONIC HARMONICA - normally the 10-hole harmonica.

DOMINANT CHORD - a 5th note above the tonic key.

DRAW NOTES - notes created by inhaling, or breathing in.

FLAT - a note that is played 1/2 step lower than the note to which it is attached.

GIG - a job to play music or entertain.

HARMONICA - harp, French harp, tin sandwich, mouth organ, pocket piano, musique abouche (French Canadian), mund harmonika (German), fisarmonica (Greek), organa de boca (Spanish).

KEY - the starting note.

LICK or RUN - a tricky pattern of notes and/or rhythms.

OCTAVE - the eight notes of any scale.

OVERBLOWING - blowing suddenly to make the reed "pop" and change pitches in an upward direction.

PITCH - the highness or lowness of a note.

POSITIONS - ability to play the harmonica in keys other than the key printed on the top plate.

RIFF - a lick on the harmonica.

SET - a performance between breaks.

SHARP - a note that is played $\frac{1}{2}$ step higher than the note to which it is attached.

SOLO - a performance where one player carries the melody of the song.

STEALING - the practice of taking something that doesn't belong to you.

STRAIGHT HARMONICA (1st Position) - playing a tune in the tonic chord (key) [playing a "C" harmonica in "C;" a "D" harmonica in "D," etc.].

SUBDOMINANT - a 4th note above the tonic key.

SYNCOPATION - cross-rhythms that occur when normally weak notes are given strong accents.

TONGUING - moving the tongue in and out on the harmonica (touching the harmonica with your tongue and then pulling it back).

TONIC CHORD - the same as the key in which you are playing.

TUNING - physically altering a harmonica to produce a new note.

VAMPING - a rhythmic accompaniment made by playing one or more notes in syncopation with the music.

VIBRATO - a vibrating of the pitch of a note.

WARBLE - a rapid movement back and forth between two or more notes.

LOWER REGISTER - holes 1, 2, 3 and 4

MIDDLE REGISTER - holes 4, 5, 6 and 7

UPPER REGISTER - holes 7, 8, 9 and 10

MAJOR SCALE - the most common scale in music. Major scales may be started on any note, but must always conform to the major scale pattern of two whole steps, one 1/2 step, three whole steps and one 1/2 step (W W H W W W H), for example, Do Re Mi Fa Sol La Ti Do

HARMONIC MINOR SCALE - the most commonly used minor scale. It raises the 7th scale step. The scale formula for the harmonic minor scale is step, 1/2 step, step, step, 1/2 step, step and a half, 1/2 step (1 - 1/2 - 1 - 1 - 1/2 - 1 1/2 - 1/2).

NATURAL MINOR SCALE (Gregorian Modes) - a scale starting on the 6th step of its Relative major scale, without any alteration.

7th HOLE - the least effective hole on the diatonic harmonica.

2nd and 3rd HOLES - the most bendable notes.

CARING FOR YOUR HARMONICA

Your harmonica, like any delicate musical instrument, requires considerable care and maintenance, and if properly done, should last for a very long time. Follow these tips:

1 - Never play after eating.

2 - Keep your harmonica clean and stored in a safe, dry place. Avoid dust, dirt, and excessive heat and moisture.

3 - If you abuse your harp by blowing too hard, the reeds may be damaged.

4 - After playing your harmonica, tap the harp against your hand to remove saliva and other moisture.

5 - Allow several hours of gentle play to "break in" a new harmonica.

6 - Brush your teeth before playing.

7 - Never soak your harmonica in any liquid. It serves no useful purpose, no matter what some of the rock players may tell you. Note: Some players believe that soaking the harmonica makes the instrument tighter thereby creating better compression and higher volume. If a wooden harmonica is soaked, the comb naturally swells and creates a tighter chamber but, it also ruins a wooden comb harmonica. Today's plastic comb harmonicas are very tight instruments anyway so I recommend that you play a plastic comb harmonica instead of soaking a wooden one. Obviously, soaking a plastic comb harp serves no purpose.

8 - Remember, abusive choking is not recommended.

9 - Periodically clean the holes in your harp with a pin or sharp pointed knife to remove built-up debris. Dried saliva will gradually accumulate around the holes and, if not dislodged, will clog them.

10 - If a reed sticks, remove the cover and carefully free it with a single-edged razor blade.

It's a good idea not to let anyone else play your harmonica since it is a very personal instrument and can be damaged very easily by a style of play to which it is not accustomed. Besides, would you share your toothbrush? The hygiene of the matter should be taken seriously.

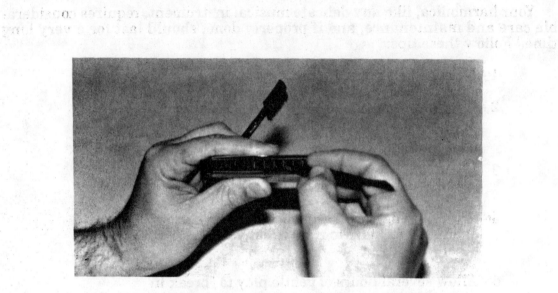

CLEANING THE HARMONICA

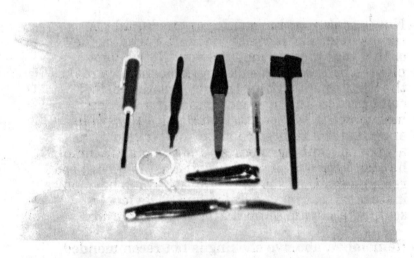

CLEANING AND REPAIR TOOLS

EXPLORING THE HARMONICA

Now that you have bought a harmonica let's see how it works. Each hole in a 10-hole, diatonic harmonica produces two notes. One note is heard when you exhale and the other when you inhale. The harmonica is constructed so that it has a top and bottom set of reeds that are sandwiched together as shown below.

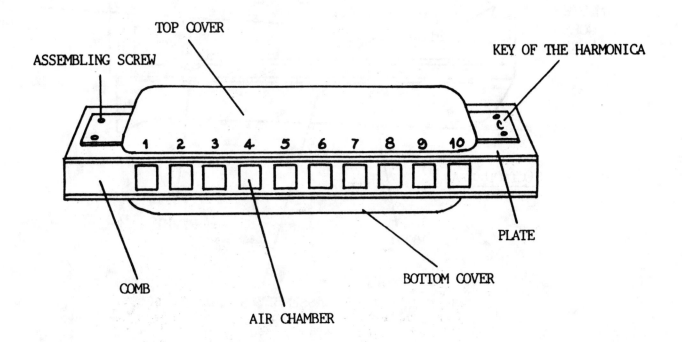

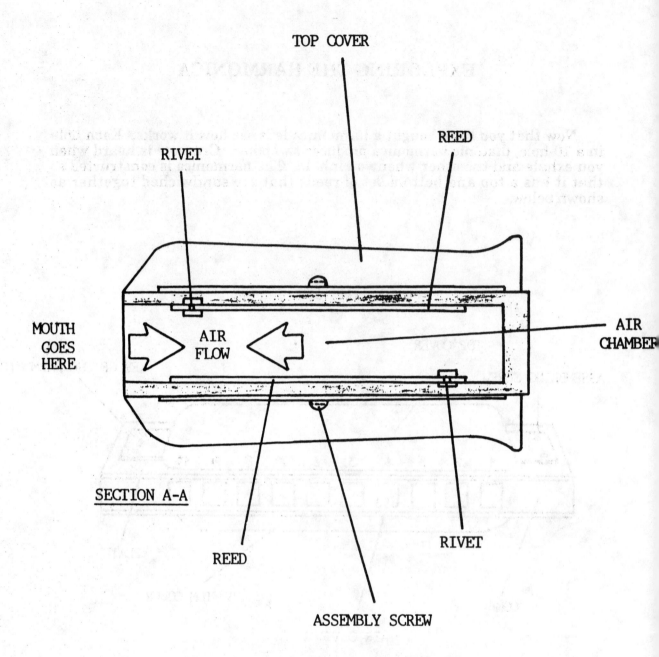

TOP COVER

REED

RIVET

MOUTH
GOES
HERE

AIR
FLOW

AIR
CHAMBER

SECTION A-A

REED

RIVET

ASSEMBLY SCREW

SECTIONAL VIEW OF A DIATONIC HARMONICA

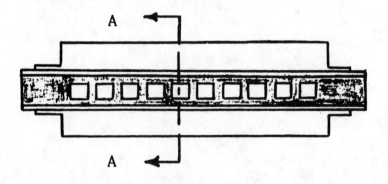

A

A

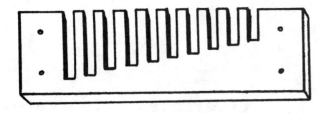

Comb - the middle part of the harmonica onto which the reed plates are assembled. Combs are made of plastic or wood.

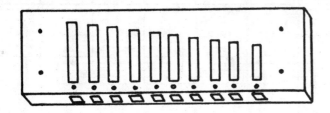

Blow Reedplate - the reeds are located on the inside of the harp and are riveted to the reedplate. The blow reed plate is located on the top of the harmonica.

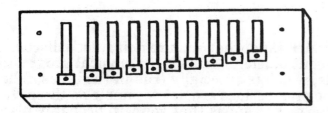

Draw Reedplate - the reeds are located on the outside of the reedplate. The draw reedplate is fastened to the bottom of the comb.

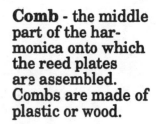

The four holes in the middle (see following illustration) contain one complete octave. This means that on your "C" harmonica you can play the complete major scale from "C" to "C," or eight total notes. As air moves through the harmonica, a musical tone is produced by the vibration of the reeds. The bigger reeds, found in the holes on the left side of the harmonica, vibrate slowly and produce a low-pitched sound. The smaller reeds, found on the right side, vibrate very rapidly, thus producing high-pitched tones. The note that is produced depends on whether you inhale or exhale and in the hole through which you blow. By carefully bending notes, the 10-hole diatonic can produce 38 notes, including chromatic notes.

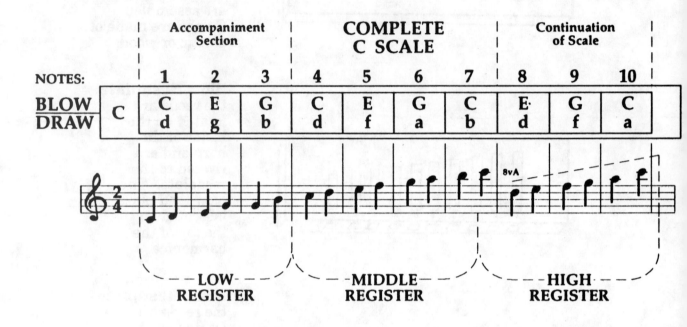

So that you can better understand what you are doing, let's discuss very briefly some simple facts about music. Basically, in musical progressions, there are three main chords, which is especially true in the blues, folk and country styles of play. Music progressions are not as simple as three chords; however, most musical patterns and tunes that you will probably play are centered around these three chords.

Tonic Chord: The same as the key in which you
are playing, for example "C."

Subdominant Chord: A 4th step above the (tonic)
key in which you are playing,
for example "F," if the tonic
chord is "C."

Dominant Chord: A 5th step above the (tonic) key
in which you are playing,
for example "G," if the tonic
chord is "C."

11

The following diagram shows these chords in the key of "C:"

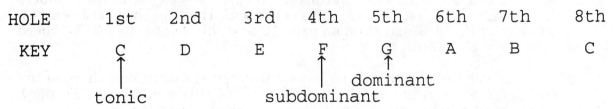

HOLE	1st	2nd	3rd	4th	5th	6th	7th	8th
KEY	C	D	E	F	G	A	B	C

tonic   subdominant   dominant

This will be true of any key in which you are playing. To find the subdominant and dominant notes, simply count up from the tonic key of your harmonica.

On every harmonica there are four notes of the same key as the harmonica, all appearing as blow notes. The illustration on page 11 is for a "C" harmonica, and as you can see, there are four "Cs" on a "C" harmonica. Each "C" note is a blow note. An "A" harmonica would have four "As," a "B" harmonica would have four "Bs," and so on. These four notes will always appear in the same location on every harmonica (blow holes 1, 4 , 7 & 10) regardless of the key of the harmonica, and will always be blow notes.

PIANO

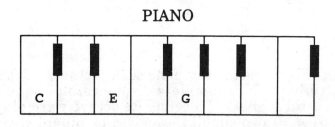

C MAJOR CHORD ON PIANO

In the following illustrations a capital letter represents a blow note and a small letter represents a draw note:

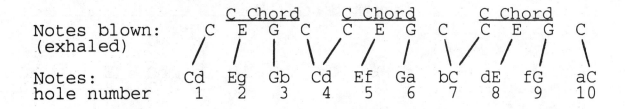

Notes blown: C E G C   C E G C   C E G C
(exhaled)

Notes: Cd Eg Gb Cd Ef Ga bC dE fG aC
hole number   1   2   3   4   5   6   7   8   9 10

By simultaneously blowing holes 1 through 4, 4 through 7, or 7 through 10, a chord of the harmonica is produced. Notice that in each case the notes blown are C E G C (on the "C" harmonica, on previous page), which produces a "C" chord on a "C" harmonica. This is the tonic chord in the chord progression. Notice in the illustration on page 12 how this relates to the "C" chord on the piano keyboard.

By drawing (inhaling) through holes 1 through 4, a dominant chord of the chord progression is produced. In the key of "C" this would be a "G" chord. Because of this 2nd position, "cross" harp is possible (see page 29).

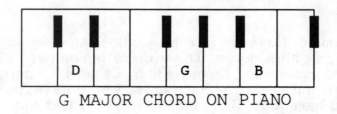

G MAJOR CHORD ON PIANO

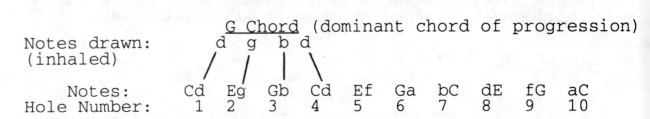

As mentioned earlier, the only complete scale (octave) on the harmonica is found in holes 4 through 7; a complete octave cannot be played (without bending) in holes 1 through 4. If a complete octave were played in holes 1 through 4, then, when drawn simultaneously, a dominant chord of the chord progression would not be produced. But rather, a discord would occur and second-position "cross" harp would not work.

Below is the only complete scale (without bending and overblowing) on the harmonica. Begin with a blow 4 and end with a blow 7.

Complete Scale of C Major

				Cd	Ef	Ga	bC		
Notes:	Cd	Eg	Gb	Cd	Ef	Ga	bC	dE	fG	aC
Hole numbers:	1	2	3	4	5	6	7	8	9	10

In all of our illustrations from this point on, a hole number with a line under it (4) indicates a "draw" (inhale) note, while a hole number without a line (4) indicates a blow (exhale) note.

13

LET'S GET STARTED

The first thing to learn is how to properly hold the harmonica, which is shown in the photographs below. I consider the "cradle" method to be the best way to hold the harmonica because you can create two types of vibratos with your hand: distinct vibratos done by opening and closing the "chamber" using your fingers, or soft vibratos with the fingers kept tightly together and the heels of the hands opening and closing slowly. The "cup" method is also commonly used in country music. When using this method the harmonica is cupped completely in the hands with the fingers of both hands pointing directly upward. Then, a catchy syncopation may be created by opening and closing the cup tightly in rhythm with the music.

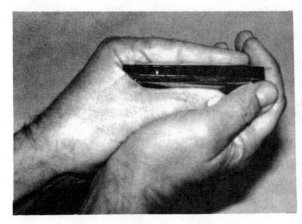 

THE "CRADLE" METHOD   THE "CUP" METHOD

When holding the harmonica the numbers should be at the top, which places the low notes on the left and the high notes on the right. Some harmonica players apparently learned to play the instrument upside down as children - and still play the same way! I once tried this after listening to one of the best "chokers" I had ever heard play that way. I theorized that perhaps having the draw reeds on the top of the harp instead of the bottom would affect one's ability to choke. After much practice I decided that it made little difference, and that that fellow was simply a good "choker."

VIBRATO CREATED WITH
THE FINGERS

VIBRATO CREATED WITH THE
HEEL OF THE HANDS

Next, you should learn to play single notes, which is probably the most important initial skill to develop in harp playing. There are basically three methods to use in learning to "hit" single notes. They are:

1 - **The Tongue Block** - This method blocks all the holes with your tongue except the one in which you wish to play. A person normally would block three holes with the tongue and leave one hole open for air passage.

2 - **The Tongue Curl**-By curling your tongue up on both sides and making the end of your tongue "U" shaped, you can direct the flow of air into only one hole.

3 - **The Pucker**-the third (and most simple and effective) style for today's Nashville sound is the pucker method. It consists of simply puckering your lips up small and oval-shaped (like an oval-shaped kiss) and opening your lips enough to blow through one hole. This is very effective because your tongue is free to bend, chord, flutter and choke, which will be very useful later on. I suggest this method.

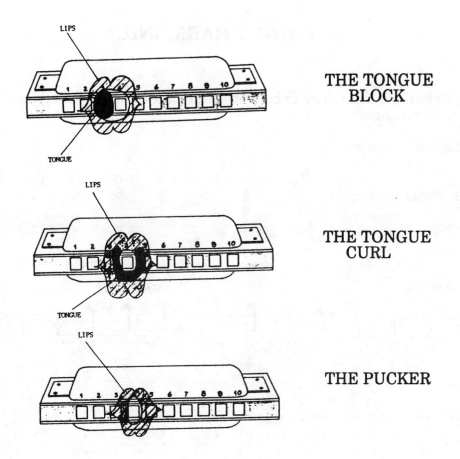

THE TONGUE
BLOCK

THE TONGUE
CURL

THE PUCKER

I alternate among all three methods; however, 95% of the time I use the pucker method. I would suggest that you develop and get into the habit of using this method since it provides much more versatility.

STRAIGHT HARMONICA

Now that you know how to hold the harmonica and position your lips, let's play the scale. Again.

The Major Scale

Notes:		Do	Re	Mi	Fa	So	La	Ti	Do
Hole Numbers:		4	4	5	5	6	6	7	7

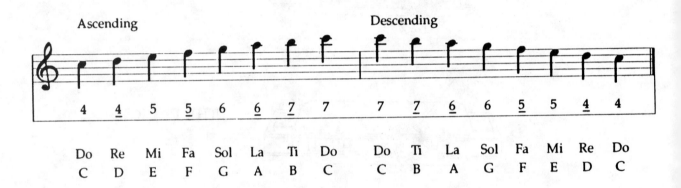

	4	4	5	5	6	6	7	7		7	7	6	6	5	5	4	4
	Do	Re	Mi	Fa	Sol	La	Ti	Do		Do	Ti	La	Sol	Fa	Mi	Re	Do
	C	D	E	F	G	A	B	C		C	B	A	G	F	E	D	C

Play the scale over and over until you can hit all notes distinctly and smoothly. Then learn to play the scale backward.

Now let's try a few simple children's tunes.
(Remember: A line under the number means draw, no line means blow.)

Mary Had A Little Lamb

```
Ma ry had a li ttle lamb    li ttle lamb   li ttle lamb
5  4  4  4  5  5   5        4  4    4       5  6    6

Ma ry had a li ttle lamb    fleece was white as snow
5  4  4  4  5  5   5        4      4    5     4  4
```

Row, Row, Row Your Boat

```
Row  row  row your boat     gent ly down the stream
4    4    4   4    5         5    4   5   5   6

Mer ri ly   mer ri ly   mer ri ly   mer ri ly
7   7  7    6   6  6    5   5  5    4   4  4

Life is but a dream
6    5  5   4  4
```

Hot Cross Buns

```
5 4 4    5 4 4    4 4 4 4 4 4 4 4    5 4 4
```

When The Saints Go Marching In

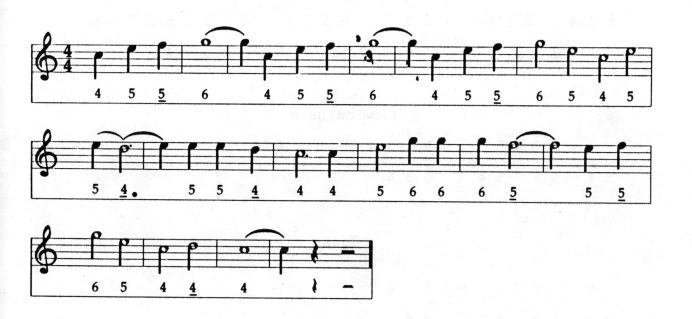

CONGRATULATIONS!! YOU'RE NOW PLAYING STRAIGHT HARMONICA!!

18

1st POSITION SONGS

Let's increase our repertoire!

Skip to My Lou

```
5 5 4 4 5 5 6      4 4 3 4 4 5      5 5 4 4 5 5 6

4 5 5 5 4 4 4      5 4 5 5 5 6          4 3 4 4 5

5 4 5 5 5 6        4 5 5 5 4 4 4
```

Three Blind Mice

```
5 4 4     5 4 4     6 5 5 5    6 5 5 5    6 7 7 7 6 7 7 6 6

6 7 7 7 6 7 7 6 6     6 7 7 7 6 7 7 6 6       5 5 4 4
```

Taps
(low on harp)

```
3 3 4    3 4 5    3 4 5    3 4 5    3 4    3    4

5 4    5 6    5 4 3    3 3 4
```

Taps
(high on harp)

```
6 6 7    6 7 8    6 7 8    6 7 8    6    7

8 7    8 9    8 7 6    6 6 7
```

19

Boil Them Cabbage Down

```
Boil them cab - bage down boys,  hoe them hoe cakes round
 5    5    5       5   5  5     5    5   5    4    4

The only song that I can sing - is boil them cabbage down.
 4   5    5     5  5 5   6      5   5    5     4   4    4
```

**(To add fullness to this song, you should keep time with the music by chord-
ing. Try to make the harp say, "Do-wacka, Do-wacka.")**

Shenandoah
('Cross the Wide Missouri)

```
O Shen-an-doah,   I love your daugh ter,
3  4   4   4      4  5    5    6     6

Roll away, you rolling river
 7   7 6    6   6  6     5 6

I'll take her cross your rolling water,
 6    6    6    6     5    6    5  4     4

Roll a-way, I'm bound a-way,
 4   4  5    4    5    6  6

'Cross the wide Miss ou ri.
  4    4    5    4    4  4
```

Cumberland Gap

```
Me - 'n my wife and my wife's pap walked all the way to the
6      5  5   4   4   5   6     6   6       5    5   4  3   3

Cumberland Gap
 4   4   4    4

Cumberland Gap, the Cumberland Gap, fifteen miles to the
 6   6   5   4   4   5   5   6    6    6    5     4     3  3

Cumberland Gap.
 4   4   4    4
```

20

Wildwood Flower

```
I will twine with my min - gle of raven black hair
5   5    6    6   7   5   5  5  4     5   4     4

With the ros - es so red and the li - lies so fair
5   5    6    6  7  5   5   5   4     5  4    4

And the myrtles so bright with its em - er - ald dew,
6   7    8    8       8   7    6    6  6   7    6   6

And the pale and the leader and eyes look like blue
4   4    5    5    4    5   6   5   4    5   4    4
```

Use tongue chording on the song above. Hold the harp using the "cup method" and open and close the cup in timing with the music.

Casey Jones

```
Come, all you rounders, if you want to hear
6    7    7    7    6    6  7   6   7  6

The story of a brave engineer
6   7 7  7  6  6   6  6 7

Casey Jones was the rounder's name
7   7    7    6   7   6   7     6

On a six eight wheeler, boys, he won his fame
5 5  6   6     6  6     6     6  5   5  4   4

Casey Jones, mounted to the cabin,
5   6    6      7  8  8   7  8 7

Casey Jones, with his orders in his hand
5   6    6    6   6   7  8  8  7    8

Casey Jones, mounted to the cabin,
5   6    6      7  8   8  7 8 7

He took his farewell trip up to the promised land.
4   4   4    5    6    6  6  6 5   5   4      4
```

21

Endings

Shave and a haircut a two bits
7   6 6 <u>6</u> 6 <u>6</u> <u>7</u>   7

Here is another popular ending (banjo ending).

6 7 7 <u>6</u> <u>7</u> <u>6</u> 6 <u>6</u> 6 <u>5</u> 5

Camptown Races

Camptown ladies sing this song, doo dah doo dah.
6 6   5 6 <u>6</u>   6   5   5 <u>4</u> 5 <u>4</u>

Camptown racetrack five miles long. Oh doo dah day.
6 6   5 6   <u>6</u> 6   5   <u>4</u> 5 <u>4</u> 4

They're gonna run all night. They're gonna run all day.
 4   4 4 5 6   7   <u>6</u>   <u>6</u><u>6</u> 7 <u>6</u> 6

Bet my money on a bob-tail nag. Somebody bet on the bay.
6 6   5 5 6   <u>6</u>   6   5   <u>4</u> 5<u>5</u> 5 <u>4</u> <u>4</u> 4

Oh Susannah

Well, I come from Alabama with my banjo on my knee
 4 <u>4</u>   5   6 <u>6</u>66 5   4 <u>4</u> 5 5 <u>4</u> 4 <u>4</u>

An' I'm going to Louisiana oh my true love for to see.
4 <u>4</u>   5 6   6 6<u>6</u>6 5   4 <u>4</u> 5   5   <u>4</u> <u>4</u> 4

Oh Susannah! Oh don't you cry for me.
<u>5</u> 5 <u>6</u> <u>6</u>   <u>6</u> 6   6   5   4 <u>4</u>

For I'm bound for Louisiana oh my true love for to see.
 4 <u>4</u>   5   6 6<u>6</u>6 5 4 <u>4</u> 5   4   <u>4</u>   <u>4</u> 4

Sewanee River

Way---down up - on the Sewan - ee river, far, far a - way
5   4 4   5 4   4   7 6 7   6   5 4   4

There's where my heart is turn - ing ev - er---There's where
5   4 4   5   4 4   7 6   7   6   5

the old folks stay.
4   4   4   4

Amazing Grace

Oh Amazing grace, how sweet the sound
3 4 4 5   5   4   4   3

That saved a wretch like me
3   4   5   5   4   6

I once was lost but now am found,
5 6   5   4   4   4   3

Was blind but now I see
3   4   5   4 4

You will notice that there are a couple of notes that do not sound exactly right but don't worry. When we play this tune in 2nd position, we'll hit all of them.

For He's A Jolly Good Fellow

For he's a jolly good fellow
4   5   5 5 4   5   5 5

For he's a jolly good fellow
5   4   4 4 4   4   5 4

For he's a jolly good fellow
4   5   5 5 4   5   5 6

Which nobody can deny
6   6 6 6 5   4 4

23

Cripple Creek

I gotta gal at the head of the creek,
7 7 7   6 5   5   5 6 6   6

Goin' up to see her about 8 times a week,
 5 5 5   5 4   4   4   5   3   3 4

Kiss her on the mouth just as sweet as any wine,
 7   7   7 7   6   5   5   5   6 6 6

Wrap her arms around me like a sweet tater vine
 5   5   5   5 4   4   4   3   3   4

Goin' up to Cripple Creek, going on a run
5 5   5   5 4 4   4   5 5   5 5 6

Goin' up to Cripple Creek to have a little fun
5 5   5   5 4 4   4 4   2 2 3 3   4

Goin' up to Cripple Creek, going in a whirl
5 5   5 5 4 4   4   5 5 5 5 6

Goin' up to Cripple Creek to see my girl
5 5   5 5 4 4   4 4 3 3 4

Dixie

Oh I wish I was in the land of cotton
 6 5 4   4   4 4 5 5   6   6 6 5

Good times there are not forgotten
 6   6   6   6 6 6 6 7

Look away, look away, look away, Dixie land
 7 8 8   7   6 7   6   5 6   4 5   4

I wish I was in Dixie, away, away
6 7   8 8   7 6 7   6 8   6 8

In Dixie land I'll take my stand to live and die in Dixie
 6 7 8   8   7   6 7 8   6 6 5   7   5 5 4

Away, away, away down South in Dixie
 5 4   5 4   6 6   5   8   8   8 7

24

Polly Wolly Doodle

Oh I went down   South for to see my gal
4 4   5   5   4   4   4 5   5 4

Singing polly wolly doodle all day
4 4   5 5 55   5   5   4

My Sal she is a spunky gal
3 4   4   3 3   4 4 3

Singing polly wolly doodle all day
4 4   6 6   6 6 5 5   4   4

Fare thee well, fare thee well
4   4   5   4   4   5

Fare thee well my fairy fay
4   4   5   5 5 5   4

For I'm bound to Louisiana for to see my Susianna
3   4   4   4 4 3 3   3   4 4   4 4 4 3 3

Singing polly wolly doodle all day
4 4   6 6   6 6   5 5   4   4

Joy to the World

Joy to the world, the Lord has come
7   7 6   6   5   5   4   4

Let Earth receive her King
6   6   6 7   7   7

Let every heart prepare for him a room
7 7 7 6 6 6 6 5 5 7 7   7   6   6 6 5 5

And heaven and nature sing, and heaven and nature sing
5   5   5   5   5 5   6   5   5   4   4   4 5   5

And heaven and heaven and nature sing
5   4 4   7   6 6   5   5 4   4

Tom Dooley

Hang down your head Tom Dooley
  6   6   6   <u>6</u>   7   8 8

Hang down your head and cry
  6   6   6   <u>6</u>   7 <u>8</u>

Hang down your head Tom Dooley
  6   6   6   <u>7</u>   8 <u>8</u> <u>8</u>

Poor boy you're bound to die
  <u>8</u> <u>8</u>   8   7   <u>6</u> 7

Red River Valley

From this valley they say you are going
  3   4   5 5   5   5   <u>4</u> 5   <u>4</u> 4

We will miss your bright eyes and sweet smile
  3 4   5   4   5   6   <u>5</u>   5   <u>4</u>

And they say you are taking the sunshine
  6 <u>5</u>   5   5   <u>4</u> 4 <u>4</u> 5   6 <u>5</u>

That has brightened our pathways awhile
  4   3   3   <u>3</u>   4   <u>4</u> 5   <u>4</u> 4

My Darling Clementine

Oh my darlin', oh my darlin', oh my darlin', Clementine.
 4 4 4 3   5 5 5 4   4 5 6 6   <u>5</u> 5 <u>4</u>

You are lost and gone forever. Dreadful sorry Clementine.
 <u>4</u> 5   <u>5</u>   <u>5</u> 5   <u>4</u> 5 4   4 5   <u>4</u> 3   <u>3</u> <u>4</u> 4

Deck the Halls

Deck the halls with boughs of holly
6   5   5   4   4   4   5 4

Fa la la la la, la la la la
4 5 5 4 5   4 4 3 4

'Tis the season to be jolly
6   5   5 4   4 4 5 4

Fa la la la la, la la la la
4 5 5 4 5   4 4 3 4

Don we now our gay apparel
4   5 5   4   5   5 6 4

Fa la la, la la la, la la la
5 5 6   6 7 7   7 6 6

Toll the ancient yule tide carol
6   5   5 4   4   4   5 4

Fa la la la la, la la la la
6 6 6 6 6   5 5 4 4

    Playing straight harmonica is simple - you simply learn blow-draw pat-
terns to fit the melody of a song. Most amateur players learn a few blow-
draw patterns, play straight harmonica, and consider themselves accomplished players. An analogy would be a person who reads one volume of an
encyclopedia and claims to be an expert on everything in the entire collection.
A person who only plays straight harmonica, which is the first step in learning to play the instrument, has barely uncovered the harmonica's potential

CROSSING AND BENDING THE HARMONICA

As discussed earlier, **cross harmonica** means playing a tune in a key other than the tonic key of the harp. It is possible to "cross key" a harp of any key so that it may be played in all other keys (positions). This means that any harmonica could possibly be played in twelve different keys, although I've never met anyone who could do it.

The most common positions are 1st (straight harmonica), 2nd, 3rd, & 4th, 5th and 12th. (For more information regarding position playing you need to purchase our advanced textbook.) Almost all Nashville-style playing is done in 2nd position so we will devote our space in this book to that position; however, 3rd position is beginning to be heard more and more.

When the term **cross harp** is used, it generally means playing a tune in the dominant key, that is playing a "C" harmonica in the key of "G", for example. To do this, most of your tunes will begin with a draw (inhale) note. This may seem difficult at first, but is really quite easy, and you'll eventually reach a point where you'll pick up your harmonica and automatically start playing in second position. Because **cross harp** is possible, you can get the blues, crying and wailing sounds on your harmonica. You will see that you can do ten times as much with a draw note as you can with a blow note. It is like pushing or pulling a rope - it's much easier to pull a rope than it is to push one. We can create notes that are not on the harmonica by drawing and "squeezing or bending," which you can't do by blowing, except on the high notes. Because of this, we want most of our notes to be draw notes, which is accomplished by playing in 2nd position.

Bending or **choking** is the art of creating notes that are not on the harmonica. To play Nashville-style, it is imperative that you become an expert at bending. Not all reeds on the harmonica are bent in the same manner: holes 1 through 6 are bent by drawing and holes 7 through 10 are bent by blowing. Hole 7 is the most inflexible of all the notes and is next to impossible to bend. The illustration on page 30 shows the notes that can be created by bending a "C" harmonica.

Note: Comical as it may seem, I have met people who thought that you bent notes by actually bending the body of the harmonica while playing. They believed that the twisting action changes the pitch of the notes. Playing in this manner serves only one purpose - it ruins a good harmonica. I also met one fellow who actually thought that playing "cross" meant playing while you were angry.

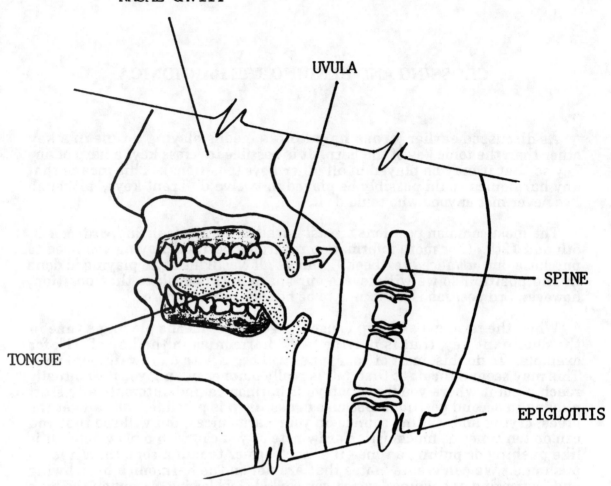

NASAL CAVITY

UVULA

SPINE

TONGUE

EPIGLOTTIS

Choking the "draw" notes is accomplished by changing the airflow across the tongue and through the mouth. As illustrated above, the uvula (little tongue) swings back and upward to close off the nasal passage while the tongue is "humped up" to squeeze the air across the harmonica reed. This causes the reed to vibrate in a slight "side-way" direction and causes the pitch of the note to drop.

The mouth is the "sound box" of the harmonica. The shape of the teeth, tongue and membranes of the mouth determine the sound the musician gets from a harmonica. As you listen to the different artists play, you will begin to notice that each one sounds a little different from the others. Aside from the artist's control of the uvula, and the artist's skills with chest, throat and hand vibratos, the tone quality of the music is very much dependent upon the structure of the musician's mouth and throat.

The illustration below is for a diatonic harmonica in the key of C.

Overblows

		Eb		Bb					
Choke notes	1½ step	Eb		Bb
or	full step		F#		B
Overblows	½ step						Eb	F	Bb
								F#	B

HOLES	1	2	3	4	5	6	7	8	9	10
BLOW	C	E	G	C	E	G	C	E	G	C
DRAW	D	G	B	D	F	A	B	D	F	A

	½ step	Db	F#	Bb	Db	E	Ab
Choke	full step		F	A			
	1½ step			Ab			

By choking and overblowing, the full chromatic scale is possible on a 10 hole diatonic harmonica.

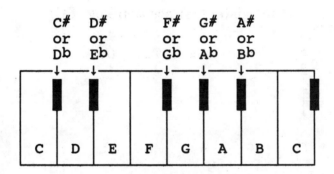

These notes are repeated up and down the keyboard

Let's practice bending so as to play the scale on the upper and lower registers. Please note the following symbols for choking.

3 - draw hole 3

3↓ - draw (choke) hole 3 ($1/2$ step down)

3↓↓ - draw (choke) hole 3 [2 half steps (1 full step) down]

3↓↓↓ - draw hole 3 (3 half steps [$1 1/2$ steps] down)

10↓↓ - blow hole 10 (2 half steps [1 full step] down)

Scale: Harmonica Lower Register (1st position-key of C)

Do	Re	Mi	Fa	Sol	La	Ti	Do
1	1	2	2↓↓	2	3↓↓	3	4
C	D	E	F	G	A	B	C

Scale: Harmonica Upper Register (1st position-key of C)

Do	Re	Mi	Fa	Sol	La	Ti	Do
7	8	8	9	9	10	10↓	10
C	D	E	F	G	A	B	C

31

LET'S PLAY CROSS HARP

See if you can figure out what position and key you are in.

Twinkle, Twinkle, Little Star

Twinkle,   twinkle little star, how I wonder where you are
2 2   4 4   5 5   4   4 4   3 3   3   3↓ 3

Up above the world so high, like a diamond in the sky
4 4 4 4   3   3 3↓   4 4 4 4 3 3 3↓

Twinkle, twinkle little star, how I wonder where you are
2 2   4 4   5 5   4   4 4   3 3   3↓ 3↓ 3

Mary Had A Little Lamb

Mary had a little lamb, little lamb, little lamb
3 3↓ 3 3↓ 3 3   3   3↓ 3↓ 3↓ 3 4   4

Mary had a little lamb, its fleece was white as snow
3↓ 3↓ 3 3↓ 3 3 3   3   3↓ 3↓ 3   3↓ 3

These are ½ step chokes on hole 3 to pick up the missing A on a C harmonica.

Yankee Doodle

Yankee Doodle went to town, a riding on a pony
<u>2</u> 2   <u>3</u> 3   <u>2</u>   <u>3</u>   <u>3</u> 1   2 2 <u>3</u> <u>3</u> <u>2</u> 2
        ↓   ↓   ↓   ↓

He stuck a feather in his hat and called it macaroni
<u>1</u> <u>2</u>   <u>2</u> <u>3</u> 3   4 <u>3</u>   <u>3</u>   2   <u>2</u>   1 2 <u>2</u> 3 3
           ↓   ↓   ↓   ↓

Yankee Doodle keep it up, Yankee Doodle dandy
2 <u>2</u>   2 <u>1</u>   2   <u>2</u> 2   1 2   <u>4</u> 4   <u>3</u> <u>4</u>
    ↓   ↓

Mind the music and your step and with the girls be handy
2   <u>2</u>   2 <u>1</u> 2   <u>2</u>   <u>2</u>   2   <u>1</u> 2   <u>2</u>   <u>3</u> 3 3
       ↓   ↓   ↓   ↓

Earlier, we learned to play "Wildwood Flower" in 1st position (straight harp), now let's learn to cross it along with the other songs that follow.

Wildwood Flower

I will twine with my mingles of raven black hair
<u>3</u>   4   <u>4</u>   5   6   <u>3</u> 4 <u>3</u> <u>3</u> <u>3</u>   <u>3</u>   3
                                    ↓   ↓

With the roses so red and the lilies so fair
<u>3</u>   4   <u>4</u> 5 6 <u>3</u>   4   <u>3</u> <u>3</u> <u>3</u>   3
                             ↓   ↓

And the myrtles so bright with its emerald dew
4   5   <u>7</u> <u>7</u>   <u>6</u> 6   <u>4</u>   <u>4</u> 5 6 5   <u>4</u>

And the pale and the leader and eyes look like blue
<u>3</u>   4   <u>4</u>   5   6   <u>3</u> 4   <u>3</u>   <u>3</u>   3   <u>3</u>   <u>3</u>
                              ↓   ↓

Amazing Grace

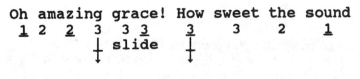

Oh amazing grace! How sweet the sound
1 2 2 3 3 3   3   3   2   1
         |slide |

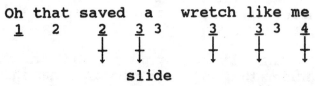

Oh that saved a   wretch like me
1   2   2   3 3   3   3 3 4

slide

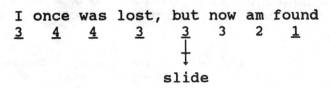

I once was lost, but now am found
3   4   4   3   3   3   2   1

slide

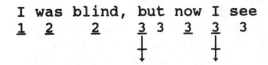

I was blind, but now I see
1 2   2   3 3 3 3 3

Here is a tune to practice some simple choking.

STEALING LICKS

The best way to learn to play the harmonica is to listen to other people play. We are fortunate today to have the high technology recording equipment to record and listen to the music that you want to learn. It is no wonder that we are seeing a higher level of musician at a much younger age than in the past. If you want to learn today you certainly have the tools to do so.

Buy all the albums that you can get with harp playing on them. To help you I have enclose a list of albums that have been helpful to me. Listen to them over and over and over...until you can repeat the licks exactly like the artist on the record. Slow down the speed of the record. Learn the licks in slow speed...then get faster.

I suggest that you buy as many keys of harmonicas as you can afford. At first I suggest that you purchase a full set (all 12 keys) of standard tuned harmonicas. This way when you hear a lick that you like...find the proper key of harmonica and learn the lick. Without all twelve keys, you will only rarely find a lick in the same key as your harmonica . Once you can afford it, you need to also buy all 12 keys of the Special Tuned (5th reed tuned 1/2 step) harmonica. If you have trouble finding all the different keys, you may purchase them from our company at the enclosed address.

Especially helpful to me is a small hand held microcassette recorder. Keep this with you and keep it ready to capture licks from the radio, T.V., etc. Be sure to purchase one with a tape speed of 2.4 sp and 1.2 lp. Always record on 2.4 sp. That way you may play the fast licks as half speed so that you can decipher the blow-draw patterns.

My philosophy: If they don't want it stolen...they had better not play it!!

PRACTICE, PRACTICE, PRACTICE!

Everyone wants to know the secret to success. There is no secret to success...no magical solution...no easy roads to the top. Success comes from doing a number of little things right over and over for an extended period of time. A person gets better at anything by constantly applying the basic principles. This text has provided you with the principles...Now the ball is in your court!

Years ago, a friend of mine wanted me to teach him how to play the harmonica. He was so carried away with his new found talents that he practiced constantly. He was determined to master the harmonica. Once in the middle of the night his wife was awakened by the muffled sound of a harmonica. She found her husband still in bed, with his back to her, his head in a pillow, facing the wall, practicing a lick that had come to him in the middle of the night. That is determination!

The principles and techniques in this text took me 15 years to learn on my own. With practice, your skills should develop at an accelerated rate. Devote extra time to the skills that are the hardest to develop and don't get discouraged. Learn to do the basic skills well and the big things will take care of themselves.

Good luck and keep on harpin'!

<u>Harmonica Seminars</u>

Ray Steelman is now available to conduct "on site" harmonica instruction seminars!

Great for:

        Harmonica Clubs
        Schools
        Community Education Programs
        Churches
        Performing Arts Festivals
        County Fairs
        Senior Centers

Now you can get "the guy who wrote the book."

For more information call:
205-379-2354

 ## <u>Attention Bookstores and Dealers</u>

Ray and Sharon Steelman are now available for autograph and promotional sessions at your bookstore locations.

Call or fax to:

Steelman Music Enterprises
(205) 379-2354

ORDER FORM

Title	Quantity		Total Price
Hyperventilation Blues	_____	X $10.00 =	_____
Loco Motion	_____	X $10.00 =	_____
Harp Attack	_____	X $10.00 =	_____
Ray Steelman and the Good, the Bad and the Ugly...Live	_____	X $10.00 =	_____
Bama Jammer	_____	X $10.00 =	_____

Al. residents add 5.5% sales tax   _____

Shipping & handling $1.50 per tape   _____

TOTAL   _____

Please forward tape(s) to:

_____
Name

_____
Address

_____
City/St/Zip

Send check or money order to:

Steelman & Associates, Inc.
7249 Winchester Road
New Market, AL 35761

(205) 379-2354